Sidney Crosby

By Jeff Savage

AMAZING ATHLETES

Lerner Publications Company • Minneapolis

Lerner Publications Company
A division of Lerner Publishing Group, Inc.
241 First Avenue North
Minneapolis, MN 55401 USA

For reading levels and more information,
look up this title at www.lernerbooks.com

Library of Congress Cataloging-in-Publication Data

Savage, Jeff, 1961–
    Sidney Crosby / by Jeff Savage.
       p.   cm. — (Amazing athletes)
    Includes bibliographical references and index.
    ISBN 978–0–7613–4054–6 (lib. bdg. : alk. paper)
    1. Crosby, Sidney, 1987– —Juvenile literature. 2. Hockey players—Canada—Biography—Juvenile literature. I. Title.
    GV848.5.C76S38 2009
    796.962092—dc22 [B]   2008026598

Manufactured in the United States of America
3 – BP – 11/1/13

TABLE OF CONTENTS

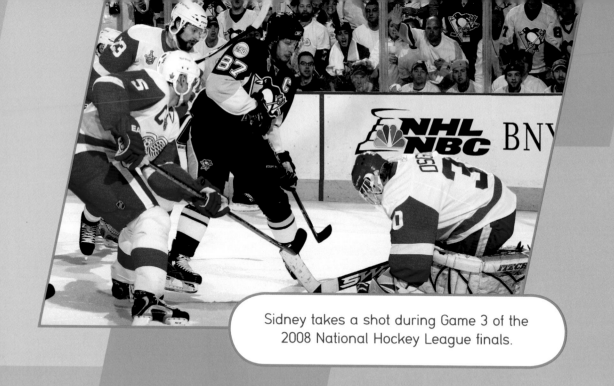

Sidney takes a shot during Game 3 of the 2008 National Hockey League finals.

REACHING A GOAL

Sidney Crosby skated up the ice in a rush. He kept the puck on the end of his stick. He cut past two **defenders**. Sidney flicked a pass through a maze of sticks to teammate Evgeni Malkin. Malkin blasted a shot toward the net. The puck sailed wide. Sidney's Pittsburgh Penguins missed again.

The Penguins were playing the Detroit Red Wings in Game 3 of the 2008 National Hockey League (NHL) finals. The first team to win four games would capture the **Stanley Cup**. The Penguins lost the first two games in Detroit. Worse yet, the Pens failed to score a goal. The Red Wings had won by scores of 4–0 and 3–0. Over 18,000 towel-waving fans packed Mellon Arena in Pittsburgh, Pennsylvania. They were hoping Sidney and his young teammates could score and win the game.

Sidney runs into Red Wings' player Nicklas Lidstrom.

The Penguins had the puck again late in the first period. Marian Hossa skated toward Red Wings goaltender Chris Osgood. Sidney smartly waited at the front of the goal. Hossa blasted a shot. Detroit defender Brad Stuart blocked it. As quick as a blink, Sidney slapped the **rebound** into the back of the net! Sidney and his teammates threw their hands in the air to celebrate. At last, they had scored a goal in the Stanley Cup finals!

Sidney cheers after scoring a goal during the first period.

The crowd cheers as Sidney celebrates with his teammates during Game 3 against the Red Wings.

Early in the second period, Pittsburgh was on the attack again. Sergei Gonchar sent the puck into the Detroit **zone**. Ryan Malone fired a shot. A Detroit skater blocked it. Sidney skated near the goal. Hossa took a shot. Osgood blocked it. But the puck skidded toward Sidney near the right post. He pounded it past Osgood for another goal! The Penguins jumped for joy as the crowd roared.

Sidney fights past two opponents to gain control of the puck.

The teams traded goals. The Penguins led, 3–1, with seven minutes left in the game. Then Detroit scored to make it 3–2. In the frantic final minutes, Sidney kept cool. He stayed close to the Detroit players. He poked his stick into plays to break up passes. The Penguins held on to win Game 3!

After the game, Penguins coach Michel Therrien praised Sidney. "There's no doubt you're looking for your best player to bring an 'A' game. Certainly Sid did that tonight." Sidney was happy with the win but knew there was still work to do. "It feels good to get a win," he said. "We definitely earned it. But it's only one."

The Penguins celebrate after winning Game 3. This important game put Sidney and his team one step closer to the Stanley Cup.

Halifax, Nova Scotia, is in the southeast corner of Canada.

SID THE KID

Sidney Crosby was born in Halifax, Nova Scotia, on August 7, 1987. Sidney grew up in the nearby town of Cole Harbour. His father, Troy, worked at a law office. Trina, his mother, worked at a grocery store. Sidney was nine years old when his sister, Taylor, was born.

Sidney's father was a hockey goalie. He was drafted by the Montreal Canadiens, but he never played in the NHL. When Sidney was two years old, his father taught him how to play. Sidney slapped pucks with a stick into the family's clothes dryer in the basement. At the age of three, Sidney began skating. Soon he was competing in hockey games against kids twice his age.

Sidney was seven when he gave his first newspaper interview. "They say you have to do your best and work hard and things will happen," he told the reporter. "You can make it if you try." Sidney practiced every day with his best friend, Jackson Johnson. He dreamed of playing in the NHL. Sidney especially liked playing goalie. "But I was told that I would have more fun chasing the puck around than standing and freezing in the net," he said.

Sidney received many prizes and awards for his skill playing hockey.

Sidney was an excellent student. He earned straight As at Astral Drive Junior High School. The vice principal called him "an amazing role model who was really kind to students in the learning center."

Sidney was a hockey **phenomenon** who never bragged about his talent. In the 2001–2002 season, he played in the triple-A midget league against older players. He scored 44 goals in 31 games. In the **playoffs**, he led the Dartmouth Subways to the title game by scoring 18 goals in five games. He was featured on the TV show *Hockey Day in Canada*. He became known as Sid the Kid. It seemed that everyone was watching Sidney.

Sidney was a star player for the Dartmouth Subways.

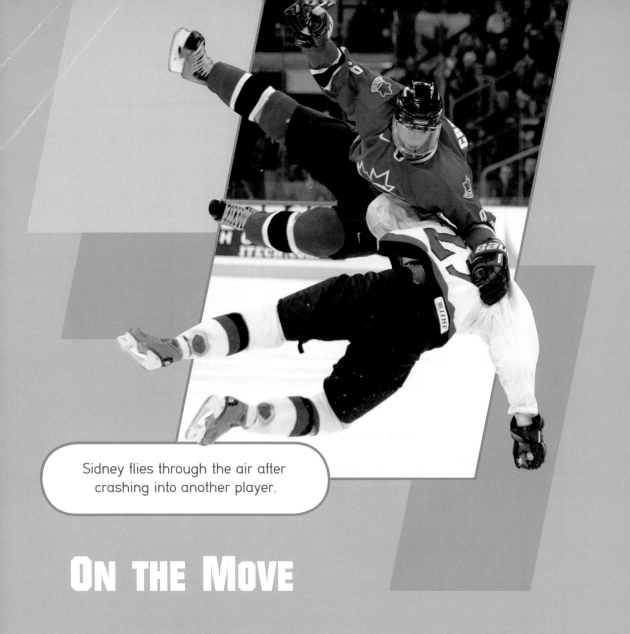

Sidney flies through the air after crashing into another player.

ON THE MOVE

As a high school **freshman**, Sidney enrolled at Shattuck-Saint Mary's School in Minnesota. It has one of the top high school hockey teams in the United States. Sidney expected to be a star for the Sabres. First, he had to make the team. Players at Shattuck had to run a mile in under six minutes. Sidney tried on his own and failed. **Personal trainer** Andy O'Brien worked with Sidney. O'Brien taught Sidney exercises to make him stronger and faster.

Sidney's fitness improved. He finished the mile in plenty of time and made the team. In 57 games at Shattuck, Sidney had 72 goals and 110 assists. He led the Sabres to the national title. In the spring, Sidney tried out for the school's baseball team. He became an ace pitcher.

Sidney moved back to Nova Scotia. He was invited to play for Canada at the World Junior Championships. He was the only player under the age of 18 to skate for the team.

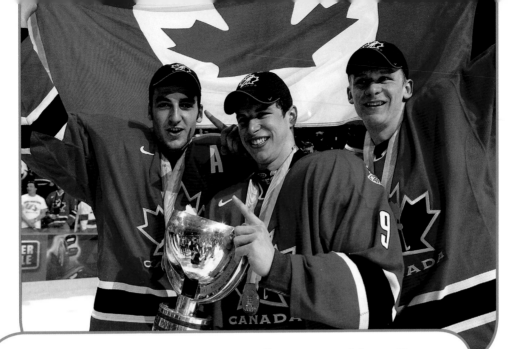

Sidney *(front)* and teammates Patrice Bergeron and Corey Perry celebrate Team Canada's victory at the World Junior Championships.

On December 28, 2003, Sidney scored a historic goal. He became the youngest player ever to score a goal for Team Canada. He was 16 years and four months old. Hockey legend Wayne Gretzky said Sidney could someday break his NHL scoring records. "If there's anyone out there who has the opportunity, he's the guy," Gretzky said. "Sidney Crosby is the best player I've seen since Mario Lemieux."

Sidney got ready to join the NHL by playing more junior hockey. He skated for two seasons for Rimouski Oceanic of the Quebec Major Junior Hockey League. Sidney skated at blazing speeds. He handled his stick like a pro. He was nearly impossible to stop. The other teams stayed close to him and knocked him into the boards. Still, Sidney was able to escape. In 121 games, he scored 120 goals and made 183 assists. He was voted the league's Most Valuable Player both years. The NHL could hardly wait for Sidney to turn pro. Sidney felt the same way.

Sidney reaches for the puck.

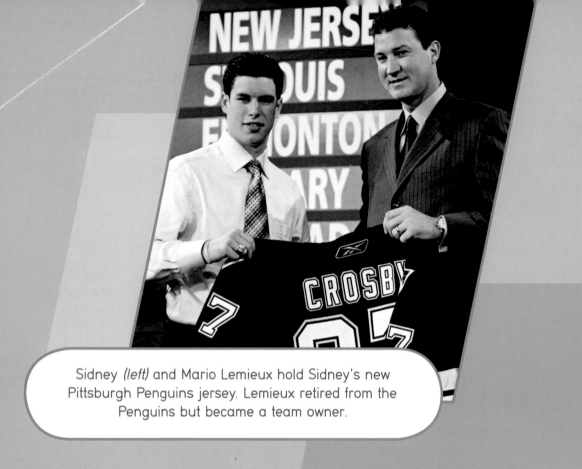

Sidney *(left)* and Mario Lemieux hold Sidney's new Pittsburgh Penguins jersey. Lemieux retired from the Penguins but became a team owner.

BREAKING THE ICE

The NHL was having troubles. Players and team owners argued about money. The 2004–2005 season was canceled. Fans were angry. Finally, the players and owners agreed to a deal. The 2005–2006 season would be played.

Everyone knew Sidney would be the first pick in the **draft**. But which team would he play for? Who would get to pick first? The order was determined by a **lottery**. Ping-Pong balls with the teams' names on them were put in a machine.

The first Ping-Pong ball to pop up was for the Pittsburgh Penguins. They picked Sidney. "I was hoping for Pittsburgh," Sidney said. "Who wouldn't want to play with Mario Lemieux?" The great Lemieux would play a few more games before retiring from hockey. And with Sidney joining the team, how could the Penguins lose? "People were talking about a Stanley Cup," Sidney said.

Sidney moved into an apartment when he joined the Penguins. Sidney grew lonely living alone. He moved in with superstar Mario Lemieux and his family.

Sidney wore jersey number 87. It was for his birth date of 8–7–87. His first pro game was against the New Jersey Devils. He got an **assist** on the team's first goal of the season scored by Mark Recchi. Sidney scored his first goal two games later against the Boston Bruins. He flicked in a rebound and shouted "Yeah!" as he fell backward. But the Pens lost again. They started the season with a record of 0–9.

Sidney was nearly six feet tall and 200 pounds. But he got pushed around by bigger NHL players. Sidney realized he had to push back. In one game, Philadelphia Flyers defenseman Derian Hatcher kicked Sidney in the face. Hatcher's skate blade knocked Sidney's front teeth out. The referees did not see what happened. Sidney shoved Hatcher. A referee blew his whistle. Sidney was sent to the penalty box for fighting.

The game went to **overtime**. Blood still dripped from Sidney's mouth. He stayed focused. He scored the game-winning goal.

Sidney was playing very well. The Penguins were not. They gave up too many goals. They missed the playoffs. Sidney finished the season with 102 points. He became the youngest player in NHL history to reach 100. But the Pens won just 22 of 82 games. "We had a rough time," Sidney said. "It was tough for me. I had never not made the playoffs at any level."

Sidney played well his first season in the NHL, but the Penguins missed the playoffs.

With Sidney's help, the Penguins were a much better team in 2006–2007.

SUPERSTAR

Sidney came out flying in 2006–2007. He was
determined to lead the Penguins to the playoffs.
In a game against the Philadelphia Flyers,
he scored three goals for his first **hat trick**.
Pittsburgh won the game, 8–2. Flyers winger
Simon Gagne said, "Sidney Crosby? You're
talking about the best player in the game."

Sidney's passing was even better than his shooting. In another game against the Flyers, he recorded five assists.

Sidney's greatest strength is his vision. He can see all the players on the ice at once. "He tells me I was open," says teammate Colby Armstrong. "I tell him I wasn't. After the game, I look at the film, and he's right." Sidney responds to all the praise by saying, "I'm just trying to get better."

Sidney always knows where his teammates are on the ice.

Sidney was named Pittsburgh's team captain for the 2007–2008 season. He was still a teenager, making him the youngest captain in NHL history. "Leadership is more doing things on the ice than talking," Sidney explained. "Actions speak louder than words. I've always tried to lead by example. Whether it's scoring a big goal or setting one up, or blocking a shot. Doing the things it takes to win a game. If you do those things, hopefully everyone will follow."

The Penguins were on track to make the playoffs. But with 11 games left, disaster struck. Against the Montreal Canadiens, Sidney blocked a puck with his foot. He crumpled to the ice in pain. His foot was broken.

Sidney refused to miss any games. Skating on a broken foot, he had five goals and nine assists in the season's final games. Pittsburgh made the playoffs for the first time in six years. Sidney finished the season with 120 points, the most in the NHL. He became the first teenager to lead the NHL in scoring since Wayne Gretzky in 1980. He was the youngest scoring champion in any major American sport in history. He was named the league's Most Valuable Player.

Sidney's skill and determination helped him set scoring records.

Sidney scores the game-winning goal
against the Ottawa Senators.

The Penguins faced the Ottawa Senators
in the 2007 playoffs. The action was intense.
Ottawa players often slammed into Sidney. The
Senators won the first game, 6–3. Sidney scored
the game-winning goal in Game 2 to even the
series. By now, he was worn out. Ottawa won
the next three games to capture the series.

Sidney was named Pittsburgh's team captain. He was just 19 years old. Many pros said he was the best hockey player in the world. Sidney proved his greatness in the 2007–2008 season. He led Pittsburgh to the playoffs again. This time, the Pens knew what to expect. They swept Ottawa in four straight games. They knocked out the New York Rangers in five games. Then they defeated the Philadelphia Flyers in the Eastern Conference finals.

Sidney led his team to the Stanley Cup finals in 2008.

In the Stanley Cup finals, the tough Detroit Red Wings won three of the first four games. They needed only one more game to win the finals. Game 5 was played in Detroit. The score was tied, 3–3, after three periods. The teams played overtime. In the third overtime period, the Penguins scored to win it! Game 6 was in Pittsburgh. The Red Wings clung to a 3–2 lead in the final moments. Sidney slapped a shot at the goal with two seconds left. The puck skidded two inches wide of the post. The final horn sounded. The Penguins had lost.

"We just came up short," Sidney said. "We have to remember this feeling." Sidney was already thinking about the next season. As the NHL's best player, he knows he will have plenty of chances to raise the Stanley Cup and celebrate.

Selected Career Highlights

2009 Led Penguins to victory in Stanley Cup finals

2008 Led Penguins to Stanley Cup finals
Named to NHL All-Star Team

2007 Won the Art Ross Trophy as the NHL's top scorer
Won the Hart Memorial Trophy as the NHL's Most Valuable Player
Named to NHL All-Star Team
Won ESPY Award as NHL's best player

2006 Set Penguins team record for assists in a season by a rookie (63)
Set Penguins record for points in a season by a rookie (102)
Youngest player in NHL history to record 100 points in a season
Youngest player to be named to NHL All-Star Team
Named to NHL All-Rookie Team

2005 Named NHL Rookie of the Month
Named Canadian Hockey League Player of the Year
Led Team Canada to the World Junior Championship
Quebec Major Junior Hockey League Most Valuable Player
Led Quebec Major Junior Hockey League in scoring

2004 Named Canadian Hockey League Player of the Year
Named Canadian Hockey League Rookie of the Year
Quebec Major Junior Hockey League Most Valuable Player
Quebec Major Junior Hockey League Rookie of the Year
Led Quebec Major Junior Hockey League in scoring

2003 Led Shattuck-Saint Mary's School to high school national title

2002 Midget Triple-A National Championship Tournament MVP Award

Glossary

assist: a pass to a teammate that helps score a goal

defenders: players whose job it is to stop the other team from scoring

draft: a yearly event in which professional teams take turns choosing new players from a selected group

freshman: a first-year student at high school or college

hat trick: a rare achievement in which one player scores three goals in a game

lottery: a game of chance in which numbers or names are picked at random

overtime: in hockey, an extra five-minute period played when a game is tied after three periods

personal trainer: a fitness expert who teaches a person exercises and proper nutrition

phenomenon: a young superstar in a sport

playoffs: a series of contests played after the regular season has ended. Teams compete to become the champion.

rebound: in hockey, another shot at the goal that follows a shot blocked by the goalie

Stanley Cup: the silver trophy awarded each year to the NHL champion

zone: an area of the ice, marked by a blue line, in which a team defends its goal

Further Reading & Websites

Doeden, Matt. *Wayne Gretzky*. Minneapolis: Twenty-First Century Books, 2008.

Foley, Mike. *Play-By-Play Hockey*. Minneapolis: Lerner Publications Company, 2000.

Hamilton, Janice. *Canada*. Minneapolis: Lerner Publications Company, 2008.

Ross, Jesse. *All-Star Sports Puzzles: Hockey*. Vancouver, BC: Raincoast Books, 2007.

Official Website of the National Hockey League
http://www.nhl.com
The official National Hockey League website provides fans with game results, statistics, schedules, and biographies of players.

Official Website of the Pittsburgh Penguins
http://penguins.nhl.com
Get the latest stats, scores, and news about the Pittsburgh Penguins from the team's official website.

Sports Illustrated Kids
http://www.sikids.com
The *Sports Illustrated Kids* website covers all sports, including hockey.

Index

Photo Acknowledgments

The images in this book are used with the permission of: © Gregory Shamus/NHLI via Getty Images, p. 4; © Jamie Sabau/Getty Images, pp. 5, 9; © Dave Sandford/Getty Images, pp. 6, 16, 29; © Bruce Bennett/Getty Images, pp. 7, 8; © age fotostock/SuperStock, p. 10; Reprinted with permission from The Halifax Herald Limited, © Tim Krochak/The Chronicle Herald, p. 12; Reprinted with permission from The Halifax Herald Limited, © Eric Wynne/The Chronicle Herald, p. 13; AP Photo/Marianne Helm, p. 14; © Jaakko Avikainen/AFP/Getty Images, p. 17; AP Photo/Jonathan Hayward, p. 18; AP Photo/Andrew Rush, p. 21; © Len Redkoles/Getty Images, p. 22; AP Photo/Mel Evans, p. 23; AP Photo/Jonathan Hayward, CP, p. 25; © Phillip MacCallum/Getty Images, p. 26; AP Photo/Keith Srakocic, p. 27.

Front Cover: © Dave Sandford/Getty Images.